CHRISTMAS AT HOME

Candy Lover's COOKBOOK

HOLIDAY RECIPES & MORE

Conover Swofford

BARBOUR
PUBLISHING

© 2008 by Barbour Publishing, Inc.

Compiled by Conover Swofford.

ISBN 978-1-60260-161-1

Scripture quotations are taken from the King James Version of the Bible.

Cover photograph: Vieussens/Canopy Photography/Veer

Published by Barbour Publishing, Inc., P.O. Box 719, Uhrichsville, Ohio 44683, www.barbourbooks.com

Our mission is to publish and distribute inspirational products offering exceptional value and biblical encouragement to the masses.

 Member of the
Evangelical Christian
Publishers Association

Printed in China.

O taste and see that the LORD is good.

PSALM 34:8

CANDY TEMPERATURES

When using a candy thermometer, make sure the thermometer does not touch the bottom of the saucepan when you are reading the temperature.

Soft ball   238°
Hard ball   248°

Contents

Fruit 7

Taffy 24

Caramels, Toffee & Butterscotch 30

Nuts 51

Coconut 69

Chocolate 81

Fudge 94

Truffles 117

Other Favorites 130

FRUIT

I saw Christmas—a tiny Babe in a manger.

I heard Christmas—the glorious song of the angels.

I felt Christmas—the peace of the Father in my heart.

Date Loaf Candy

2½ cups sugar
1 cup milk
⅛ teaspoon salt
1 tablespoon butter

½ teaspoon baking soda
1 cup chopped dates
1 cup chopped pecans

In saucepan, boil sugar, milk, and salt until mixture forms soft ball when dropped in cold water. Add butter. Mix well. Add baking soda and chopped dates. Beat with wooden spoon until mixture is cool. Add chopped pecans. Shape into roll. Cut into slices approximately 1 inch thick. Store in tightly covered container.

Chocolate Date Nut Rolls

1 pound crushed graham crackers,
  divided
1 pound diced dates
1 pound mini marshmallows

2 cups chopped walnuts
2 cups whipping cream,
  whipped
4 squares semisweet
  baking chocolate

Set aside ½ cup crushed graham crackers. Fold remaining crushed graham crackers, dates, marshmallows, and walnuts into whipped cream. Form mixture into rolls and roll in reserved crumbs. Wrap rolls in plastic wrap and chill overnight. Melt chocolate squares in small saucepan over low heat, stirring constantly. Pour melted chocolate over date nut rolls. Chill for at least 1 hour. Cut into slices approximately 1 inch thick. Store in tightly covered container in refrigerator.

Jesus is the true star of Christmas,
who by His life and words still lights the way
for those who are seeking God.
We live by the light of His counsel.

Caramel Apples

5 medium apples
5 wooden skewers
1 (14 ounce) package caramel
    candies, unwrapped

¼ cup corn syrup
¾ cup chopped walnuts

Spray small cookie sheet with cooking spray and set aside. Wash and dry apples. Insert skewer into stem end of apples. In small bowl, microwave caramels and corn syrup on high for 3 to 4 minutes, stirring every minute until caramels are melted and smooth. Dip apples in hot caramel mixture, turning to coat well. Allow caramel to drip from apples, scraping excess from bottom of apples. Roll bottom of apples in walnuts. Place on prepared cookie sheet. Refrigerate for at least 1 hour.

Date-Fig Confections

1 pound figs
1 pound dates

1 pound almonds
Powdered sugar

Chop figs, dates, and almonds in food processor. Pour mixture onto cutting board covered with powdered sugar. Work with your hands until well blended. Roll to ¼-inch thickness, using powdered sugar on rolling pin to prevent sticking. Cut into ¾-inch squares. Roll each piece in powdered sugar and shake off excess. Pack in layers between waxed paper in tightly covered tin.

Chocolate-Dipped Strawberries

1 cup semisweet chocolate chips
½ cup white chocolate chips
1 tablespoon oil

2 pints fresh strawberries,
rinsed and patted dry

In microwavable bowl, melt semisweet and white chocolate chips and oil on high for 1 minute. Stir. Melt on high for 30 seconds or until completely melted. Holding top, dip bottom two-thirds of each strawberry in melted chocolate mixture. Shake gently to remove excess. Place on tray lined with waxed paper. Refrigerate for 1 hour or until coating is firm. Cover. Store in refrigerator.

White Chocolate Apricots

½ cup white chocolate chips,   20 dried apricot halves
    melted

Dip each apricot half in melted chocolate, coating both sides. Place on waxed paper. Cool. Store in refrigerator.

Cherry Chocolate Logs

1 cup semisweet chocolate chips
¼ cup sweetened condensed milk
¼ teaspoon almond extract

½ cup maraschino cherries
1 cup pecan pieces

In microwavable bowl, melt chocolate chips on high for 1 minute. Stir. Melt on high for 30 seconds or until completely melted. Stir in condensed milk and almond extract. Stir in cherries. Refrigerate until mixture can be shaped into logs, about 15 minutes. Shape mixture into 2 logs. Roll logs in pecan pieces. Refrigerate until firm. Cut into ½-inch slices. Store in refrigerator.

Cherry Vanilla Nougat

2 cups sugar
½ cup sour cream
⅓ cup light corn syrup
2 tablespoons butter
¼ teaspoon salt

1 cup chopped walnuts
½ cup chopped maraschino
   cherries
2 teaspoons vanilla

In 3-quart saucepan, combine sugar, sour cream, corn syrup, butter, and salt. Bring to a boil over medium heat, stirring constantly. Boil for 5 minutes. Remove from heat. Let stand for 15 minutes. Stir in walnuts, cherries, and vanilla. Spread into 8x8-inch buttered pan. Refrigerate 2 hours. Cut into squares.

Glacé Cherries

2 cups sugar
1 cup boiling water

⅛ teaspoon cream of tartar
8 ounces maraschino cherries

In small saucepan, combine sugar, water, and cream of tartar. Heat over high heat until boiling, stirring to keep mixture from sticking. When mixture reaches a boil, remove from heat and immediately place saucepan in larger pan filled with cold water to stop boiling. Remove saucepan from cold water and place in another pan of hot water during dipping. Drain juice from cherries. Using dipping spoon, dip cherries one by one into syrup. Place 1 inch apart on waxed paper. Allow to cool. Store in tightly covered container in refrigerator.

Banana Clusters

1 (12 ounce) package semisweet
   chocolate chips
⅓ cup peanut butter

1 cup unsalted peanuts
1 cup banana chips

Put chocolate chips and peanut butter in large microwavable bowl. Microwave on high for 2 minutes, stirring after 1 minute, or until chips are melted and mixture is smooth. Fold in peanuts and banana chips. Drop by rounded teaspoonfuls onto waxed paper that has been sprayed with butter-flavored nonstick cooking spray. Refrigerate until firm. Store in tightly covered container in refrigerator.

Candy Apples

2 cups sugar
⅔ cup light corn syrup
1 cup water
¼ teaspoon cinnamon

Red food coloring (optional)
5 medium apples, with
    wooden skewers inserted in
    stem end of each

In saucepan, combine sugar, corn syrup, water, and cinnamon. Cook, stirring constantly, over medium heat until sugar is dissolved. Bring to a boil. Cover and cook for 3 minutes until steam has washed away any crystals on sides of pan. Uncover and cook without stirring until candy thermometer reads 290°. Remove from heat. Pour into top of double boiler over hot but not boiling water. Add a few drops of red food coloring if desired. Working quickly, dip each apple in candy mixture. Turn apples to coat thoroughly. Scrape off excess candy. Stand apples on waxed paper. Allow to harden.

Apricot Balls

8 ounces dried apricots
1 cup flaked coconut

¼ cup sweetened condensed
milk
Additional flaked coconut

Chop apricots in food processor. Add coconut and process until combined. Add condensed milk and process until combined. Pour into pie pan. Refrigerate until firm enough to shape into balls—about 30 minutes. Place additional coconut in shallow pan. Shape mixture into 1-inch balls. Roll balls in coconut. Place on baking sheet lined with waxed paper. Refrigerate until firm. Store in refrigerator.

Sugarplums

½ cup white chocolate chips
¼ cup light corn syrup
½ cup chopped dates
¼ cup chopped maraschino cherries

1 teaspoon vanilla
1¼ cups crushed gingersnaps
Flaked coconut

In small saucepan, melt chocolate chips with corn syrup, stirring constantly. Stir in dates, cherries, and vanilla. Blend well. Add gingersnaps, stirring until blended. Mixture will be stiff. Form mixture into ¾-inch balls and roll in coconut. Place in small foil cups. Let stand overnight to allow flavors to blend.

Chocolate-Covered Cherries

2½ cups semisweet chocolate chips, divided
1 tablespoon butter

36 maraschino cherries with juice

In small saucepan over low heat, melt chocolate chips with butter, stirring constantly. Spoon about ½ tablespoon chocolate mixture into 36 small foil cups. With back of spoon, spread chocolate up sides of each cup, forming hollow center. Refrigerate until firm. Place 1 cherry and a little juice in each chocolate cup. Cover with melted chocolate. Refrigerate until firm. Store in refrigerator.

Chocolate-Covered Raisins

1 cup milk chocolate chips
⅓ cup sweetened condensed
  milk

1 teaspoon vanilla
2 cups raisins

In saucepan, melt chocolate chips with condensed milk and vanilla over low heat, stirring occasionally. Remove from heat. Stir in raisins. Drop by teaspoonfuls onto baking sheet lined with buttered waxed paper. Refrigerate until firm.

TAFFY

How to Pull Taffy

Pour taffy mixture onto cutting board covered with powdered sugar. Let cool. Be careful as center of mixture might still be hot enough to burn. Butter your fingers. Pick up handful of taffy mixture. Pull to about 8 inches long. Fold in half and pull to 8 inches again. Repeat until candy is opaque in color and only slightly sticky. Roll into rope about 1 inch in diameter and let cool. Repeat until all taffy is pulled.

Taffy

2 tablespoons butter
2 cups sugar

½ cup vinegar
Powdered sugar

In saucepan, melt butter over low heat. Add sugar and vinegar. Cook over medium heat until sugar is dissolved. Boil until candy thermometer reaches 248°. Pour onto cutting board covered with powdered sugar. When cool enough to handle, pull until candy is porous. Roll into rope with 1-inch diameter. Allow to cool. Cut into 1-inch pieces.

Velvet Taffy

1 cup molasses
3 cups sugar
1 cup boiling water
3 tablespoons vinegar

½ teaspoon cream of tartar
½ cup melted butter
¼ teaspoon baking soda
Powdered sugar

In saucepan, combine molasses, sugar, water, and vinegar. Bring to a boil. Add cream of tartar. Stirring constantly, boil until candy thermometer reaches 248°. Add butter and baking soda. Remove from heat. Stir to blend thoroughly. Pour onto cutting board covered with powdered sugar. When cool enough to handle, pull until candy is light colored. Roll into rope with 1-inch diameter. Allow to cool. Cut into 1-inch pieces.

Taffy Delight

2 cups molasses   ¼ teaspoon baking soda
1 tablespoon vinegar

In saucepan, combine molasses, vinegar, and baking soda. Cook over medium heat, stirring constantly until candy thermometer reaches 248°. Remove from heat and stir in baking soda. Beat until mixture looks light and foamy. Pour into buttered pan and let set until cool enough to handle. Butter hands and pull half the taffy at a time until it hardens and loses its stickiness. Roll into rope with 1-inch diameter and let cool completely. Break or cut into bite-sized pieces and wrap in waxed paper.

Molasses Taffy

2 cups molasses
⅔ cup sugar
3 tablespoons butter

1 tablespoon vinegar
Powdered sugar

In saucepan, melt together molasses, sugar, and butter. Cook over medium heat until sugar is dissolved, stirring constantly. Boil until candy thermometer reads 248°. Add vinegar and immediately remove from heat. Pour onto cutting board covered with powdered sugar. When cool enough to handle, pull until candy is light colored. Roll into rope about 1 inch in diameter. Allow to cool. Cut into 1-inch pieces.

Butter Taffy

2 cups light brown sugar
¼ cup molasses
2 tablespoons vinegar
2 tablespoons water

¾ teaspoon salt
¼ cup butter
2 teaspoons vanilla

In saucepan, combine brown sugar, molasses, vinegar, water, and salt. Boil until candy thermometer reads 248°. Remove from heat. Add butter. Stir until butter is completely melted and blended. Add vanilla. Mix well. Pour into buttered 8x8-inch pan. Cool. Cut into squares.

CARAMELS, TOFFEE & BUTTERSCOTCH

[Mary] brought forth her firstborn son, and wrapped him in swaddling clothes, and laid him in a manger; because there was no room for them in the inn.

LUKE 2:7

Chocolate Toffee

1 cup butter
1 cup brown sugar
1 cup pecan pieces

1 (6 ounce) package milk
   chocolate chips

In saucepan, melt butter and brown sugar over low heat, stirring constantly. Let boil for 10 minutes. Spread pecan pieces into greased 9x13-inch pan. Pour butter–brown sugar mixture over nuts. When set but still warm, sprinkle chocolate chips on top and allow to melt. When completely cooled, cut into 1-inch pieces.

Sultana Caramels

¼ cup butter
2 cups sugar
½ cup milk
¼ cup molasses

½ cup semisweet chocolate
chips
½ cup walnut pieces
2 tablespoons sultana raisins
1 teaspoon vanilla

In saucepan, melt butter over low heat. Add sugar, milk, and molasses. Bring to a boil. Boil for 7 minutes. Add chocolate chips and stir until chocolate is melted. Boil for another 7 minutes. Remove from heat. Beat on medium speed until creamy. Add walnuts, raisins, and vanilla. Stir to mix. Pour into buttered 8x8-inch pan. Cool. Cut into squares.

Butterscotch Delights

1½ cups mini marshmallows
1 cup pecan pieces
2 cups butterscotch chips

½ cup sweetened condensed milk

Butter 9x13-inch pan. Spread marshmallows and pecan pieces evenly on bottom of pan. In saucepan, combine butterscotch chips and condensed milk. Stir constantly over low heat until chips are melted. Pour mixture over marshmallows and nuts in pan. Use spatula to spread mixture evenly. Let stand at room temperature until set. Cut into squares. Refrigerate.

Chocolate Caramels

2½ tablespoons butter
2 cups molasses
1 cup brown sugar
½ cup whole milk

1 square semisweet baking
   chocolate, chopped
1 teaspoon vanilla

In saucepan, combine butter, molasses, brown sugar, and milk. Cook over low heat until butter is melted and mixture is blended well. Add chocolate. Stirring constantly, heat until chocolate is completely melted. Boil until candy thermometer reads 248°. Remove from heat. Add vanilla. Blend completely. Pour into buttered 8x8-inch pan. Cool. Cut into squares.

Butterscotch Caramels

1 cup butter, cut into pieces
2½ cups light brown sugar
½ cup dark corn syrup

¼ cup light corn syrup
1 cup heavy cream
2 teaspoons vanilla

In saucepan over low heat, stir butter, brown sugar, and both corn syrups until sugar is dissolved. Bring to a boil over medium heat and cook until candy thermometer reaches 248°. Remove from heat. With wooden spoon, gradually add cream. Over medium heat, bring mixture back to a boil. Cook until candy thermometer reaches 248°. Remove from heat. Stir in vanilla. Pour into buttered 9x13-inch pan. Let stand until set. When cool, cut into pieces.

Butterscotch

2 cups sugar
⅔ cup dark corn syrup

¼ cup water
¼ cup heavy cream

In saucepan, combine all ingredients. Stir over low heat until sugar is dissolved. Raise heat to medium and bring to a boil. Boil until candy thermometer reaches 300°. Pour candy into buttered 9x13-inch pan. Let cool. Score into 1-inch squares. When cooled completely, break into pieces.

Butterscotch Divinity

2 cups sugar
½ cup light corn syrup
⅓ cup water
2 egg whites

⅛ teaspoon cream of tartar
1 teaspoon vanilla
½ cup butterscotch chips
½ cup pecan pieces

In saucepan, combine sugar, corn syrup, and water. Cook over medium heat, stirring constantly until sugar dissolves and mixture comes to a boil. Continue to cook until mixture reaches 255°. Remove from heat. Beat egg whites and cream of tartar on high speed until stiff peaks form. Gently add hot syrup mixture, beating constantly. Add vanilla. Beat until soft peaks form. Stir in butterscotch chips and pecans. Drop by tablespoonfuls onto baking sheet lined with waxed paper. Store in refrigerator.

Jesus was God's presence come to dwell with humankind, as well as God's present, the hope of humankind.

Haystacks

1½ cups peanut butter   1 cup pretzel sticks
3 cups butterscotch chips

Melt peanut butter and butterscotch chips over low heat. Remove from heat.
Pour over pretzel sticks. Stir to coat. Drop by teaspoonfuls onto waxed paper.
Cool.

Caramel Popcorn

¼ cup butter
½ cup light corn syrup
1 cup brown sugar
⅔ cup sweetened condensed
   milk

1 teaspoon vanilla
5 cups popped corn,
   unpopped hulls removed

Combine butter, corn syrup, and brown sugar. Bring to a boil. Stir in condensed milk and return to a boil, stirring constantly. Remove from heat and stir in vanilla. Pour over popped corn and stir to coat. With buttered hands, form into balls. Place on waxed paper to set. Makes about 15 popcorn balls.

Christmas Caramels

2 cups sugar
2 cups light corn syrup
1 cup half-and-half

1 cup butter
1 cup whipping cream
1 teaspoon vanilla

In saucepan, combine sugar, corn syrup, half-and-half, and butter. Bring to a boil over medium heat, stirring occasionally. Boil for 25 minutes or until temperature reaches 245°. Remove from heat. Gradually stir in cream. Return to medium heat. Cook 15 minutes or until mixture reaches 248°. Remove from heat. Stir in vanilla. Pour into 8x8-inch pan lined with buttered foil. Cool at room temperature at least 4 hours. Remove from pan. Place on cutting board. Cut into 1-inch squares. Store in tightly covered container at room temperature.

Almond Butter Toffee

1 cup slivered almonds   ½ cup sugar
½ cup butter   1 tablespoon light corn syrup

In 10-inch skillet, combine all ingredients. Bring to a boil over medium heat, stirring constantly. Continue boiling, stirring constantly until mixture turns golden brown. Spread candy into 9x9-inch pan lined with buttered foil. Cool thoroughly. Break into pieces.

The true miracle of Christmas is
not only that the mighty God, Creator of
all the universe, chose to become a baby,
but that He chooses to live in our hearts.

Hawaiian Toffee

3½ ounces macadamia nuts,
   coarsely chopped
1 cup butter
1 cup sugar
2 tablespoons water

¼ teaspoon salt
¼ teaspoon vanilla
½ cup milk chocolate chips
1 cup toasted coconut

Line 9x9-inch pan with foil, pressing foil into corners. Spread nuts evenly in single layer on bottom of pan. In saucepan, combine butter, sugar, water, and salt. Bring to a boil over medium heat, stirring occasionally. Boil until candy thermometer reaches 305°, stirring frequently. Remove from heat. Stir in vanilla. Immediately pour over nuts in pan. Cool completely, about 30 minutes. In microwavable bowl, melt chocolate chips on high for 1 minute. Stir. Melt on high for 30 seconds more or until completely melted. Spread chocolate evenly over toffee. Top with toasted coconut. Refrigerate about 30 minutes or until chocolate is set. Bring to room temperature. Break toffee into pieces. Store in container at room temperature between sheets of waxed paper.

Toffee

1 cup pecan pieces   1 cup butter
1½ cups brown sugar   1 teaspoon vanilla

Spread pecan pieces on buttered baking sheet. Set aside. In saucepan, cook brown sugar and butter until candy thermometer reads 290°. Remove from heat and stir in vanilla. Pour over pecan pieces. Let cool completely. Break into pieces.

Turtles

1 cup pecan halves
36 caramels, unwrapped

½ cup milk chocolate chips,
melted

Preheat oven to 325°. Arrange pecan halves flat side down in clusters of four on greased cookie sheet. Place 1 caramel on each cluster of pecans. Heat in oven until caramels soften, about 4 to 8 minutes. Remove from oven. Flatten caramels slightly. Cool briefly then remove from pan to waxed paper. Swirl melted chocolate on top.

Christmas Crunchies

1 (6 ounce) package butterscotch
  chips

½ cup crunchy peanut butter
5 cups crisp rice cereal

In saucepan, stir butterscotch chips and peanut butter over low heat until butterscotch melts. Pour mixture over cereal in large bowl. Stir gently until cereal is completely coated. Drop by teaspoonfuls onto waxed paper. Chill in refrigerator for at least 2 hours.

Caramels

½ cup butter
2 cups sugar
2 cups dark corn syrup

1 tablespoon vanilla
⅛ teaspoon salt
2 cups whipping cream

In saucepan, bring all ingredients except whipping cream to a boil over medium heat until mixture is clear—about 5 minutes. Very slowly stir in whipping cream. Boil until candy thermometer reaches 248°. Pour into buttered 9x13-inch pan. Score into squares. Cool.

Caramel Nut Cups

2 cups semisweet chocolate chips
1 tablespoon butter
¾ cup pecan pieces

¾ cup caramel ice cream
  topping

In small saucepan over low heat, melt chocolate chips with butter, stirring constantly. Spoon about ½ tablespoon mixture into 36 small foil cups. With back of spoon, spread chocolate up sides of each cup, forming hollow center. Refrigerate until firm. Mix pecan pieces with caramel ice cream topping. Spoon mixture into chocolate cups. Refrigerate.

NUTS

Christmas is God's expression of Himself
wrapped in a blanket in a manger.

Christmas Peanuts

½ cup semisweet chocolate chips   ¼ cup dry roasted peanuts
½ cup butterscotch chips

In glass bowl, microwave chocolate and butterscotch chips on high for 1 minute.
Stir. Microwave for 30 seconds more or until chips are completely melted. Stir in
peanuts. Coat well. Drop by spoonfuls onto waxed paper. Let cool.

Christmas Pralines

1 cup brown sugar
½ cup sugar
½ cup heavy cream
¼ cup light corn syrup

1 tablespoon butter
1 teaspoon vanilla
1½ cups pecan pieces

In saucepan, combine sugars, cream, and corn syrup. Stirring frequently, bring to a boil over medium heat. Reduce heat to low. Cook until candy thermometer reaches 238°. Remove from heat. Add butter and vanilla. Beat with wooden spoon for 1 to 2 minutes or until mixture begins to thicken. Stir in pecans. Coat nuts well. Drop mixture by tablespoons onto baking sheet lined with waxed paper. Allow to cool. Store in tightly covered container with waxed paper between layers of pralines.

Peanut Butter Cups

2 cups semisweet chocolate chips
1 cup milk chocolate chips
1½ cups powdered sugar

1 cup creamy peanut butter
½ cup graham cracker crumbs
6 tablespoons butter, softened

In microwavable bowl, melt semisweet and milk chocolate chips on high for 1 minute. Stir. Melt on high for 30 seconds more or until completely melted. Line 12 muffin cups with foil cups. Spoon approximately 1 tablespoon chocolate mixture into each cup. With back of spoon, spread chocolate up sides of each cup. Refrigerate until firm, about 20 minutes. Combine powdered sugar, peanut butter, graham cracker crumbs, and butter in medium bowl. Beat on medium speed until well blended. Spoon 2 tablespoons peanut butter mixture into each chocolate cup. Spread about 1 tablespoon remaining chocolate over each peanut butter cup. Refrigerate until firm.

Peanut Butter Crunchies

½ cup light corn syrup   ½ cup crunchy peanut butter
½ cup sugar   4 cups crisp rice cereal

In saucepan, combine corn syrup and sugar. Bring to a boil over medium heat
and boil for 1 minute, stirring occasionally. Remove from heat. Stir in peanut
butter until mixture is smooth. Pour over cereal in bowl. Stir to coat well. Press
evenly into buttered 8x8-inch pan. Cool about 15 minutes. Invert onto cutting
board. Cut into 1-inch bars.

Peanut Nougat

2 cups sugar   2 cups chopped peanuts

In 10-inch skillet, melt sugar to a syrup over low heat, stirring constantly. As soon as sugar is syrupy, add peanuts and stir quickly to coat. Remove from heat. Pour at once into warmed and buttered 8x8-inch pan. Allow to cool. Cut into squares.

Creamed Walnuts

1 egg white, room temperature
½ tablespoon cold water
¾ teaspoon vanilla

2 cups powdered sugar
1 cup walnut pieces

Place egg white, water, and vanilla in bowl. Beat with mixer on medium speed until well blended. Add powdered sugar gradually, continuing to beat until mixture is stiff enough to knead. Shape into balls. Roll balls in walnut pieces. Place on waxed paper. Store in refrigerator.

Glacé Nuts

2 cups sugar
⅛ teaspoon cream of tartar

1 cup boiling water
2 cups pecan halves

In saucepan, combine all ingredients. Bring to a boil. Without stirring, boil until candy thermometer reaches 310°. Remove from heat. Place saucepan in pan of warm water to keep syrup from cooling while dipping nuts. Using dipping spoon, dip half of each pecan in syrup. Place on buttered waxed paper. Cool. Store at room temperature.

Peanut Butter Delights

1½ cups nonfat dry milk
1 cup crunchy peanut butter
1 cup honey

1 cup flaked coconut
1 cup graham cracker crumbs

Combine milk, peanut butter, honey, and coconut in medium bowl. Stir until well blended. Refrigerate until firm enough to shape into balls, about 3 minutes. Shape into 1-inch balls. Place graham cracker crumbs in small bowl. Roll balls in crumbs. Place on baking sheet lined with waxed paper. Refrigerate until set. Store in refrigerator.

Bull's Eyes

½ cup crunchy peanut butter
6 tablespoons butter, softened
1 tablespoon light corn syrup
1 teaspoon vanilla
2 cups powdered sugar

1 cup graham cracker crumbs
¾ cup semisweet chocolate
   chips
2 tablespoons shortening

Beat peanut butter, butter, corn syrup, and vanilla on medium speed until smooth. Beat in sugar and crumbs on low speed until well mixed. Mixture will look dry. Shape into 1-inch balls. In microwavable bowl, melt chocolate chips and shortening on high for 1 minute. Stir. Melt on high for 30 seconds more or until completely melted. With dipping spoon, dip peanut butter balls in chocolate mixture. Place on baking sheet lined with waxed paper. Let chocolate set completely before storing in tightly covered container.

Cashew Brittle

2 cups milk chocolate chips
¾ cup coarsely chopped cashews
½ cup butter, softened

½ cup sugar
2 tablespoons light corn syrup

Line 9x9-inch pan with foil. Butter foil. Spread chocolate chips evenly over bottom of pan. In saucepan, combine cashews, butter, sugar, and corn syrup. Cook over low heat, stirring constantly until butter is melted and sugar is dissolved. Continue to cook over medium heat until mixture begins to cling together and turns golden brown. Pour mixture over chocolate chips in pan, spreading evenly. Cool. Refrigerate until firm. Remove from pan. Break into pieces. Store tightly covered in a cool, dry place.

God sent His Amazing Grace to earth
to be born in a stable in Bethlehem.

Spiced Nuts

1 cup powdered sugar
½ teaspoon cinnamon
¼ teaspoon nutmeg

½ teaspoon salt
2½ tablespoons oil
2 cups nuts of your choice

Stir together powdered sugar, cinnamon, nutmeg, and salt. Pour oil in skillet and heat. Add half of dry mixture and heat slowly, stirring constantly until sugar is dissolved and thickened. Add nuts and mix until coated with spiced syrup. Combine nut mixture with remaining dry mixture. Mix until nuts are completely covered. Let cool.

Microwave Brittle

1 cup sugar	1 teaspoon butter
½ cup light corn syrup	1 teaspoon vanilla
1½ cups dry roasted peanuts	1 teaspoon baking soda

In 2-quart microwavable bowl, stir sugar and corn syrup until well mixed. Microwave on high for 7 to 8 minutes or until syrup is pale yellow. Stir in peanuts. Microwave on high for 1 to 2 minutes or until nuts are lightly browned. Immediately stir in butter, vanilla, and baking soda, stirring until foamy. Pour onto buttered cookie sheet. Spread evenly. Cool. Break into pieces.

Almond Brittle

1¾ cups sugar
⅓ cup light corn syrup
¼ cup water

1 cup butter
1½ cups finely chopped
almonds

In saucepan, combine sugar, corn syrup, and water. Bring to a boil over medium heat, stirring constantly. Cover. Cook for 1 minute. Remove cover. Add butter. Stirring constantly, cook until candy thermometer reads 290°. Remove from heat. Stir in almonds until just blended. Pour into buttered 10½x15½x1-inch jelly roll pan. Cool completely. Break into pieces.

Traditional Peanut Brittle

2 cups sugar
2 tablespoons light corn syrup
1 cup water
1 cup peanuts

1 teaspoon baking soda
⅛ teaspoon salt
2 tablespoons butter

Combine sugar, corn syrup, and water; cook to 290° on candy thermometer. Remove from heat. Add peanuts, baking soda, salt, and butter. Stir quickly. Pour onto greased baking sheet and spread thin. When cool, break into pieces.

Peanut Brittle

1½ cups salted peanuts
1 cup sugar
1 cup light corn syrup

¼ cup water
2 tablespoons butter
¼ teaspoon baking soda

Place peanuts in ungreased 8x8-inch pan and warm in oven at 250°. In saucepan, combine sugar, corn syrup, water, and butter. Stir over medium heat until sugar is dissolved and temperature reaches 280°. Gradually stir in warm peanuts. Keep cooking until temperature reaches 300°, stirring frequently. Remove from heat. Stir in baking soda until thoroughly blended. Pour onto heavily buttered cookie sheet. Spread evenly. Cool about 30 minutes or until set. Break into pieces.

Pecan Roll

1 cup heavy cream
2 cups sugar
1 cup brown sugar

½ cup light corn syrup
2 cups pecan pieces

In saucepan over medium heat, cook cream, sugars, and corn syrup until heated to 238°. Remove from heat and allow to cool slightly. Beat until creamy. Knead until firm. Shape into roll. Roll in pecan pieces until thoroughly covered. Place on waxed paper. Allow to cool completely. When firm, cut into 1-inch slices.

COCONUT

Glory to God in the highest, and on
earth peace, good will toward men.

LUKE 2:14

Coconut Haystacks

2 cups sugar
1 cup brown sugar
¾ cup water

1 cup dark corn syrup
½ teaspoon salt
4½ cups flaked coconut

In saucepan over low heat, cook sugars, water, corn syrup, and salt until sugar is dissolved. Turn heat up to medium. Stirring constantly, cook until mixture reaches 238°. Remove from heat. Stir in coconut. Mix thoroughly. Drop by tablespoons onto waxed paper. When cool, store in tightly covered container.

The Magi did not exchange gifts among themselves but presented everything to the Son of God. How do you honor the Christ who gave up everything to become our Savior?

Choco-Coconut Bars

Crust:
    1 cup flaked coconut   ½ cup butter, melted

Topping:
    1 (4 ounce) package coconut   1 cup pecan pieces
    1 (14 ounce) can sweetened   1 (6 ounce) package semisweet
      condensed milk   chocolate chips

Mix coconut with melted butter. Spread in bottom of 8x8-inch pan. Bake at 300° for 25 minutes. Mix coconut, condensed milk, and pecan pieces. Pour mixture onto crust and spread evenly. Sprinkle chocolate chips on top. Bake at 350° for 30 minutes or until chocolate is melted. Remove from oven. Cool completely. Cut into 1-inch bars.

Coconut Almond Delights

¾ cup cream cheese, softened
4½ to 5½ cups powdered
  sugar

1 cup slivered almonds
1 cup flaked coconut
½ teaspoon coconut extract

Butter 8x8-inch pan. Beat cream cheese with enough powdered sugar to make stiff but not dry mixture. Stir in almonds, coconut, and coconut extract. Press mixture into pan. Refrigerate until firm. Cut into squares. Store in refrigerator.

Coconut Cream Candy

2 teaspoons butter
1½ cups sugar
½ cup whole milk

⅓ cup flaked coconut
½ teaspoon vanilla

In saucepan, melt butter over low heat. Add sugar and milk. Stir until sugar is dissolved. Heat to boiling and boil for 12 minutes. Remove from heat. Add coconut and vanilla. Beat on medium speed until mixture is creamy. Pour into buttered 8x8-inch pan. Cool. Cut into squares.

Coconut Almond Bars

2 cups powdered sugar
1 cup flaked coconut
⅓ cup plus 1 tablespoon sweetened
   condensed milk
1 teaspoon vanilla

1 cup slivered almonds
½ cup milk chocolate chips
½ cup semisweet chocolate
   chips
1 tablespoon butter

Combine powdered sugar, coconut, condensed milk, vanilla, and almonds in medium bowl. Stir with wooden spoon until thoroughly blended. Press into buttered 8x8-inch pan. Melt chocolate chips with butter in small saucepan over low heat, stirring constantly. Spread evenly over coconut mixture in pan. Refrigerate until almost firm. Cut into bars. Store in refrigerator.

Coconut Balls

½ cup chopped golden raisins
½ cup chopped pitted dates
½ cup graham cracker crumbs
½ cup powdered sugar

1 tablespoon orange zest
½ cup sweetened condensed
milk
1 cup flaked coconut

Combine raisins, dates, graham cracker crumbs, powdered sugar, and zest in medium bowl. Stir in condensed milk. Refrigerate until firm enough to shape into balls, about 30 minutes. Shape into 1-inch balls. Roll in coconut. Store in refrigerator.

Coconut Bonbons

1 (14 ounce) can sweetened
   condensed milk
½ cup butter
2 teaspoons vanilla
2 cups powdered sugar

2 cups flaked coconut
1 cup pecan pieces
2 (12 ounce) packages
   semisweet chocolate chips

In saucepan, combine condensed milk and butter. Cook over low heat until butter melts and mixture is blended. Remove from heat. Stir in vanilla. Put 2 cups powdered sugar in large bowl. Pour milk mixture over sugar. Beat on medium speed until blended and creamy. With wooden spoon, stir in coconut and pecan pieces until thoroughly mixed. Cover bowl with plastic wrap. Refrigerate 1 hour. Shape coconut mixture into 1-inch balls. Place on cookie sheet lined with waxed paper. Refrigerate until firm.

In large microwavable bowl, melt chocolate chips on high for 1 minute. Stir. Melt for 30 seconds more or until chips are completely melted. Dip coconut balls into melted chocolate. Remove excess chocolate by scraping bottom of bonbon across rim of bowl. Place bonbons on waxed paper. Let stand in cool place until chocolate is set. (Do not refrigerate.) Store in airtight container at room temperature.

Brown Sugar Coconut Delights

2¾ cups brown sugar
3 tablespoons light corn syrup
1¼ cups evaporated milk
3 tablespoons butter

1¼ cups flaked coconut
⅛ teaspoon salt
1 teaspoon vanilla

In saucepan, combine brown sugar, corn syrup, and evaporated milk. Mix well. Cook to 238° on candy thermometer. Remove from heat and add butter. Cool until lukewarm. Beat until thick and creamy. Add coconut, salt, and vanilla. Mix well. Pour into buttered 8x8-inch pan. When cool, cut into squares.

CHOCOLATE

The wonder of Christmas is expressed in
the wonderful love of God, who gave us the
most wonderful gift of all—His Son.

Rocky Road Delights

2 cups milk chocolate chips
¼ cup butter
1 teaspoon vanilla

1 cup mini marshmallows
2 cups chopped walnuts

In double boiler, slowly melt milk chocolate chips and butter. Remove from heat. Stir in vanilla, marshmallows, and nuts. Mix thoroughly. Pour into buttered 8x8-inch pan. Refrigerate until firm.

Layered Chocolate Mints

¾ cup semisweet chocolate chips
¾ cup white chocolate chips

1 teaspoon peppermint extract
¾ cup milk chocolate chips

In microwave-safe bowl, melt semisweet chocolate chips on high for 90 seconds or until melted. Pour into 8x8-inch pan lined with foil. Spread evenly. Allow to cool completely. Let stand until firm. In microwave-safe bowl, melt white chocolate chips on high for 90 seconds or until melted. Stir in peppermint extract. Mix thoroughly. Pour white chocolate mixture over semisweet chocolate. Spread evenly. Allow to cool completely. Let stand until firm. In microwave-safe bowl, melt milk chocolate chips on high for 90 seconds or until melted. Pour over white chocolate. Spread evenly. Cool. Refrigerate for at least 2 hours. Remove from pan. Cut into 2-inch squares.

Choco-Peanut Butter Bars

1 cup butter, softened
4 cups powdered sugar
1 cup crunchy peanut butter

1 cup graham cracker crumbs
1 (12 ounce) package semisweet
    chocolate chips

In mixing bowl, blend butter, powdered sugar, peanut butter, and crumbs. Press into buttered 9x13-inch baking pan. In microwavable bowl, melt chocolate chips on high for 1 minute. Stir. Heat for 30 seconds more or until completely melted. Spread evenly over peanut butter mixture. Chill until chocolate is firm.

Chocolate Coconut Bonbons

2 cups powdered sugar
3 tablespoons evaporated milk
2 tablespoons butter, softened
1 cup flaked coconut

1 teaspoon vanilla
1 cup semisweet chocolate
  chips
1 tablespoon oil

In medium bowl, combine powdered sugar, evaporated milk, butter, coconut, and vanilla. Shape into 1-inch balls. Place on baking sheet lined with waxed paper. Refrigerate until firm. In microwavable bowl, melt chocolate chips and oil on high for 1 minute. Stir. Melt on high for 30 seconds more or until completely melted. Dip bonbons into melted chocolate. Remove excess chocolate by scraping bottom of bonbon across rim of bowl. Place on waxed paper. Refrigerate until firm. Store in refrigerator.

Chocolate Nut Squares

¾ cup semisweet chocolate chips
¾ cup milk chocolate chips
3 tablespoons butter, divided

1 (14 ounce) package caramels
3 tablespoons whole milk
2 cups pecan pieces

In small saucepan over low heat, melt semisweet and milk chocolate chips with 1 tablespoon butter. Spoon half the chocolate mixture into 8x8-inch pan lined with buttered foil. Spread evenly across bottom and ¼ inch up sides. Refrigerate until firm. In medium saucepan, combine caramels, 2 tablespoons butter, and milk. Cook over medium heat, stirring constantly, until caramels are melted. When mixture is smooth, stir in pecan pieces. Cool to lukewarm. Spread over chocolate mixture in pan. Over very low heat, melt remaining chocolate mixture again, stirring constantly. Spread over caramel layer. Cool. When firm, cut into squares. Store in refrigerator.

Chocolate Peppermints

¾ cup semisweet chocolate chips
¾ cup milk chocolate chips

½ cup crushed peppermint
candy

In microwavable bowl, melt semisweet and milk chocolate chips on high for 1 minute. Stir. Melt on high for 30 seconds more or until chocolate is completely melted. Stir in crushed candy. Pour into buttered 8x8-inch pan. Let stand until firm. Cut into squares.

Chocolate Popcorn

2 cups sugar
½ cup light corn syrup
2 squares semisweet baking chocolate

1 cup water
4 quarts popped corn

In saucepan, mix sugar, corn syrup, baking chocolate, and water. Cook over medium heat until candy thermometer reaches 248°. Pour syrup over popped corn and mix thoroughly. Form popped corn into balls and place on waxed paper to cool.

Chocolate Pretzels

1 cup semisweet chocolate chips   2 cups mini pretzels
½ cup white chocolate chips

In microwavable bowl, melt semisweet and white chocolate chips on high for
1 minute. Stir. Melt on high for 30 seconds more or until completely melted.
Gently stir in mini pretzels and coat thoroughly. Place pretzels on baking sheet
lined with waxed paper. Let stand at room temperature until chocolate is set.

Chocolate Drops

2 egg whites, room temperature
¼ teaspoon cream of tartar
⅛ teaspoon salt
⅔ cup sugar

2 tablespoons cocoa
¾ teaspoon almond extract
2 tablespoons mini semisweet
chocolate chips

Preheat oven to 200°. Line 2 large cookie sheets with foil. In small bowl with mixer on high speed, beat egg whites, cream of tartar, and salt until soft peaks form. Still beating at high speed, add sugar 2 tablespoons at a time. Add cocoa and almond extract. Beat until stiff peaks form. Drop by level teaspoons onto cookie sheets. Sprinkle each drop with two or three mini chocolate chips. Bake for 1 hour and 15 minutes or until set. Cool for 10 minutes. With spatula, carefully loosen and remove drops from foil. Cool completely on wire racks. Store in tightly covered container. Makes 3 dozen.

Chocolate Butter Crunch

1 cup butter
1¼ cups sugar
¼ cup water
2 tablespoons light corn syrup

½ teaspoon vanilla
1 cup ground almonds,
    divided
¾ cup milk chocolate chips

In saucepan, melt butter over medium heat. Add sugar, water, and corn syrup. Bring to a boil, stirring constantly. Cook until candy thermometer reads 290°, stirring frequently. Remove from heat. Stir in vanilla and ⅔ cup almonds. Spread mixture into a 10½x15½x1-inch jelly roll pan lined with buttered foil. Let stand for 1 minute. Sprinkle with chocolate chips. Let stand for 2 to 3 minutes more until chocolate melts. Smooth melted chocolate over candy. Sprinkle with remaining ground almonds. Cool completely. Break into pieces. Store in tightly covered container.

Chocolate Cream Candy

2 cups sugar
⅔ cup whole milk
1 tablespoon butter

½ cup semisweet chocolate
   chips
1 teaspoon vanilla

In saucepan, combine sugar, milk, and butter. Cook over low heat until butter is melted and sugar is dissolved, stirring constantly. Bring to a boil. Add chocolate chips. Stir constantly until chocolate is completely melted. Boil for 13 minutes. Remove from heat. Add vanilla and beat on medium speed until mixture is creamy. Pour into buttered 8x8-inch pan. Cool. Cut into squares.

FUDGE

Christmas is the season for kindling the fire of hospitality
in the hall, the genial flame of charity in the heart.

WASHINGTON IRVING

Mississippi Mud Fudge

1 (12 ounce) package semisweet
  chocolate chips
1 (14 ounce) can sweetened
  condensed milk

1½ teaspoon vanilla
1½ cups mini marshmallows
1 cup peanuts
1 cup chopped walnuts

In saucepan, melt chocolate chips and condensed milk, stirring constantly. Remove from heat. Stir in vanilla, marshmallows, and nuts. Spread into 8x8-inch pan lined with waxed paper. Chill until firm. Remove from pan. Cut into 1-inch squares.

Christmas Fudge

½ cup whipping cream
½ cup light corn syrup
2¼ cups semisweet chocolate chips

1½ cups powdered sugar
1½ teaspoons vanilla

In saucepan, bring cream and corn syrup to a boil over medium heat. Boil for 1 minute, stirring constantly. Add chocolate chips. Cook until chocolate is melted, stirring constantly. Remove from heat. Stir in powdered sugar and vanilla. Mix thoroughly. Pour into foil-lined 8x8-inch pan. Spread mixture evenly. Cover. Refrigerate for 2 hours or until firm.

Peanut Butter Fudge

½ cup whipping cream
½ cup light corn syrup
2¼ cups peanut butter chips

1½ cups powdered sugar
1½ teaspoons vanilla

In saucepan, bring cream and corn syrup to a boil over medium heat. Boil for 1 minute, stirring constantly. Add peanut butter chips. Cook until chips are melted, stirring constantly. Remove from heat. Stir in powdered sugar and vanilla. Mix thoroughly. Pour into foil-lined 8x8-inch pan. Spread mixture evenly. Cover. Refrigerate for 2 hours or until firm.

Cookie Dough Fudge

⅓ cup butter, melted
⅓ cup brown sugar
¾ cup flour
½ teaspoon salt, divided
1⅓ cups mini semisweet chocolate
   chips, divided

2 cups powdered sugar
1 (8 ounce) package cream
   cheese, softened
1 teaspoon vanilla

In small bowl, combine butter and brown sugar. Stir in flour and ¼ teaspoon salt. Stir in ⅓ cup chocolate chips. Form dough into ball. Place on waxed paper. Flatten dough into disk. Wrap in foil. Freeze for 10 minutes or until firm. Unwrap dough. Cut into ½-inch pieces. Refrigerate. In large mixing bowl on low speed, beat powdered sugar, cream cheese, vanilla, and remaining ¼ teaspoon salt until mixed. Beat on medium until smooth, scraping sides of bowl with spatula while beating. Melt remaining 1 cup chocolate chips in microwavable bowl on high for 1 minute. Stir. Melt for 30 seconds more or until completely melted. Add melted chocolate to cream cheese mixture. Stir with wooden spoon until completely blended. Stir in chilled cookie dough pieces. Spread evenly in buttered 8x8-inch pan. Refrigerate until firm. Cut into squares. Store in refrigerator.

Fabulous Fudge

½ cup light corn syrup
⅓ cup evaporated milk
3 cups semisweet chocolate chips

¾ cup powdered sugar
2 teaspoons vanilla
1 cup walnut pieces

In saucepan, combine corn syrup and evaporated milk. Stir until well blended. Cook over medium heat until mixture boils. Remove from heat immediately. Stir in chocolate chips. Heat slowly over low heat, stirring constantly until chips are melted. Remove from heat. Stir in powdered sugar, vanilla, and walnuts. Beat until thick and glossy. Spread into 8x8-inch pan lined with foil. Refrigerate overnight.

Everything about Jesus is wonderful—
His birth, His life, His death,
His resurrection. And because of Jesus
we have wonderful hope for the future.

Double Peanut Butter Chocolate Fudge

½ cup light corn syrup
⅓ cup evaporated milk
18 ounces semisweet chocolate chips
¾ cup powdered sugar

⅓ cup crunchy peanut butter
2 teaspoons vanilla
⅓ cup creamy peanut butter

In saucepan, combine corn syrup and evaporated milk. Stir until well blended. Cook over medium heat until mixture boils. Remove from heat immediately. Stir in chocolate chips. Cook slowly over low heat, stirring constantly until chips are melted. Remove from heat. Stir in powdered sugar, crunchy peanut butter, and vanilla. Beat until thick and glossy. Spread into 8x8-inch pan lined with foil. Spoon creamy peanut butter onto fudge mixture and swirl to marbleize. Refrigerate overnight.

Honey Butter Fudge

4 cups sugar, divided
1 cup water, divided
2 egg whites, stiffly beaten

1 cup honey
⅔ cup peanut butter
1 teaspoon vanilla

Combine 1 cup sugar and ½ cup water in saucepan. Over medium heat, bring to a boil until mixture reaches 238° on candy thermometer. Add slowly to stiffly beaten egg whites and beat until stiff. In another saucepan, combine 3 cups sugar, honey, peanut butter, and ½ cup water. Over medium heat, cook until mixture reaches 238°. Beating constantly, add to first mixture slowly. Beat until stiff and creamy. Add vanilla. Pour into buttered 9x13-inch pan. Let cool. Cut into squares.

Never Fail Fudge

4 (12 ounce) packages semisweet
   chocolate chips
⅓ cup butter

1 (14 ounce) can sweetened
   condensed milk
1 (7 ounce) jar marshmallow
   crème

In saucepan over low heat, melt chocolate chips and butter. Remove from heat. Stir in condensed milk and marshmallow crème. Press mixture into buttered 8x8-inch pan. Cool. Cut into squares.

Cocoa Fudge

3 cups sugar	1½ cups whole milk
⅔ cup cocoa	¼ cup butter
⅛ teaspoon salt	1 teaspoon vanilla

In 4-quart saucepan, combine sugar, cocoa, salt, and milk. Cook over medium heat, stirring constantly until mixture comes to a boil. Boil until mixture reaches 234° on candy thermometer. Remove from heat. Add butter and vanilla. Do not stir. Let stand until temperature cools to 110°. Beat with wooden spoon until fudge thickens. Spread into buttered 8x8-inch pan. Cool completely. Cut into squares. Store in tightly covered container at room temperature.

Mocha Fudge

1 tablespoon instant coffee
1 tablespoon boiling water
2½ cups sugar
½ cup butter
1 (5 ounce) can evaporated milk

1½ cups semisweet chocolate
  chips
1 (7 ounce) jar marshmallow
  crème
½ teaspoon vanilla

Dissolve coffee in boiling water. Set aside. In saucepan, combine sugar, butter, and evaporated milk. Bring to a boil over medium heat, stirring constantly. Boil for 5 minutes. Remove from heat. Stir in coffee mixture, chocolate chips, marshmallow crème, and vanilla. Pour into buttered 9x9-inch pan. Let stand at room temperature for 1 hour. Cut into 1-inch squares. Cover. Refrigerate until fudge is set.

Peanut Butter Fudge #2

2¼ cups dark brown sugar
½ cup evaporated milk
2 tablespoons butter

¾ cup crunchy peanut butter
1 teaspoon vanilla

Butter 5x9-inch loaf pan. In saucepan, combine brown sugar, evaporated milk, and butter. Bring to a boil, stirring constantly, until sugar is dissolved. Continue boiling for 5 minutes, stirring constantly. Cool for 10 minutes. Add peanut butter and vanilla. Stir until well blended. Pour into prepared pan. Refrigerate for at least 3 hours.

Double-Decker Fudge

¾ cup peanut butter chips
¾ cup semisweet chocolate
  chips
2¼ cups sugar

1 (7 ounce) jar marshmallow
  crème
¾ cup evaporated milk
¼ cup butter
1 teaspoon vanilla

Put peanut butter chips in medium bowl and chocolate chips in another medium bowl. In saucepan, combine sugar, marshmallow crème, evaporated milk, and butter. Cook over medium heat, stirring constantly, until mixture comes to a boil. Boil for 5 minutes, stirring constantly. Remove from heat. Add vanilla. Mix thoroughly. Immediately pour half of mixture over peanut butter chips. Stir until chips are melted. Spread into bottom of buttered 8x8-inch pan. Pour other half of mixture over chocolate chips. Stir until chips are melted. Spread over peanut butter chip mixture in pan. Cool to room temperature. Chill until firm. Cut into 1-inch pieces. Store in tightly covered container at room temperature.

Turtle Fudge

1 (12 ounce) package semisweet
  chocolate chips
2 squares semisweet baking chocolate,
  chopped
1 cup sweetened condensed milk

¼ teaspoon salt
30 caramels, unwrapped
1 tablespoon water
40 pecan halves

Butter 7x11-inch pan. In saucepan, combine chocolate chips, baking chocolate, condensed milk, and salt. Stir over low heat until chocolate is melted and mixture is smooth. In small saucepan over low heat, cook caramels with water until caramels are melted. Mix caramels with chocolate mixture. Stir until smooth. Pour into prepared pan. Let stand at room temperature until firm. Cut into 40 squares. Top each square with pecan half. Store in refrigerator.

Quick Fudge

1 (12 ounce) package semisweet
    chocolate chips
1 (14 ounce) can sweetened
    condensed milk

1½ teaspoons vanilla
1 cup chopped walnuts

In saucepan over low heat, melt chocolate chips and condensed milk, stirring constantly. Remove from heat. Stir in vanilla and walnuts. Spread into 8x8-inch pan lined with waxed paper. Chill until firm. Remove from pan. Cut into 1-inch squares.

Walnut Fudge

1 quart whipping cream
1 cup dark corn syrup

4 cups sugar
1½ pounds shelled English
walnuts

In saucepan, mix whipping cream, corn syrup, and sugar. Boil until candy thermometer reaches 235°. Stir frequently. Remove from heat and beat with mixer on high until stiff. Stir in walnuts. Pour into buttered 9x13-inch pan. Cool completely. Cut into 1-inch squares.

Maple Fudge

1 cup half-and-half
¾ cup maple syrup
½ cup heavy cream
3 cups sugar

¼ cup dark corn syrup
⅛ teaspoon salt
3 tablespoons butter, softened
2 teaspoons vanilla

In saucepan, combine half-and-half, maple syrup, cream, sugar, corn syrup, and salt. Stir over low heat until sugar is dissolved. Raise heat to medium. Cook until candy thermometer reaches 238°. Remove from heat. Add butter and vanilla. Allow to sit on top of mixture until butter is melted; then stir in. Pour into buttered 8x8-inch pan. Cool for at least 1 hour. Score into 1-inch squares. Refrigerate overnight.

Layered Fudge

¾ cup semisweet chocolate chips
1 (14 ounce) can sweetened
    condensed milk, divided
1 teaspoon vanilla

1 cup mini marshmallows
1 (12 ounce) package
    butterscotch chips
½ cup pecan pieces

In microwavable bowl, melt chocolate chips on high for 1 minute. Stir. Melt on high for 30 seconds more or until completely melted. Stir in ¾ cup condensed milk and vanilla. Stir until smooth. Add marshmallows. Mix thoroughly. Pour into buttered 8x8-inch pan. Refrigerate until firm. In microwavable bowl, melt butterscotch chips on high for 1 minute. Stir. Melt on high for 30 seconds more or until completely melted. Stir in remaining condensed milk until smooth. Add pecan pieces. Cool mixture to room temperature. Spoon over chocolate layer in pan. Score into squares. Refrigerate until firm. Store in refrigerator.

Fudgy Peanut Butter Balls

2 cups milk chocolate chips
¼ cup half-and-half

⅓ cup crunchy peanut butter
⅓ cup chopped peanuts

In saucepan over low heat, melt chocolate chips with half-and-half, stirring occasionally. Whisk in peanut butter until blended. Refrigerate until mixture is firm enough to form balls—about 30 minutes. Shape mixture into 1-inch balls. Spread peanuts on waxed paper. Roll balls in peanuts. Store in refrigerator in tightly covered container.

TRUFFLES

Mine eyes have seen thy salvation,
which thou hast prepared before the face of all people;
a light to lighten the Gentiles,
and the glory of thy people Israel.

Luke 2:30–32

Coconut Cream Truffles

2 cups semisweet chocolate chips
¼ cup whipping cream
¼ cup butter

3 tablespoons coconut milk
Powdered sugar

In saucepan, melt chocolate chips with cream and butter over low heat, stirring constantly. Remove from heat. Stir in coconut milk. Refrigerate until mixture is thick but soft, about 2 hours. Shape into 1-inch balls. Place on waxed paper. Let set. Put powdered sugar in small bowl. Roll balls in sugar. If sugar won't stick because balls are set, roll balls in your hands to soften them slightly, then roll in sugar. Store in refrigerator.

Christmas Chocolate Truffles

1 (8 ounce) package cream cheese,
    softened
3 cups powdered sugar
1 (12 ounce) package semisweet
    baking chocolate, melted

½ teaspoon vanilla
1 cup finely chopped pecan
    pieces

Beat cream cheese until smooth. Gradually add powdered sugar, beating until well blended. Add melted chocolate and vanilla. Mix well. Refrigerate for about 1 hour. Shape into 1-inch balls. Roll in pecan pieces. Store in refrigerator.

Eggnog Truffles

2 cups semisweet chocolate chips
3 tablespoons butter, divided

2 cups milk chocolate chips
½ cup eggnog

In small saucepan over low heat, melt semisweet chocolate chips with 1 tablespoon butter, stirring constantly. Spoon about ½ tablespoon chocolate mixture into each of 36 small foil cups. With back of spoon, spread chocolate up sides of each cup, forming hollow center. Refrigerate until firm.

In saucepan, combine milk chocolate chips, eggnog, and 2 tablespoons butter. Melt over low heat, stirring frequently. Pour into pie pan. Refrigerate until mixture is thick but soft, about 2 hours. Spoon truffle mixture into pastry bag fitted with large star tip. Pipe mixture into chocolate cups. Refrigerate until firm.

White Chocolate Truffles

1 (12 ounce) package white
   chocolate chips
⅓ cup whipping cream

2 teaspoons orange extract
1 teaspoon orange zest
1 cup powdered sugar

In saucepan over low heat, melt chocolate chips with cream, stirring constantly. Whisk in extract and zest until blended. Pour into pie pan. Refrigerate until mixture is thick but soft, about 2 hours. Shape mixture into 1-inch balls. Roll in powdered sugar. Place in small foil cups.

Orange Truffles

¾ cup semisweet chocolate chips
2 squares unsweetened baking
   chocolate, chopped
1½ cups powdered sugar
½ cup butter, softened

1 tablespoon orange zest
1 tablespoon orange extract
2 squares semisweet baking
   chocolate, chopped

In microwavable bowl, melt semisweet chocolate chips and unsweetened baking chocolate on high for 1 minute. Stir. Melt on high for 30 seconds more or until completely melted. In bowl, beat together powdered sugar, butter, zest, and orange extract until combined. Beat in melted chocolate. Pour into pie pan. Refrigerate for 30 minutes or until mixture can be formed into balls. Shape into 1-inch balls and place on waxed paper. In microwavable bowl, melt semisweet baking chocolate on high for 1 minute. Stir. Melt on high for 30 seconds more or until completely melted. Dip balls into melted chocolate. Place on waxed paper. Cool completely. Store in tightly covered container in refrigerator.

Raspberry Truffles

2 cups semisweet chocolate chips
¾ cup sweetened condensed
  milk

¼ cup raspberry jam
2 tablespoons butter
½ cup white chocolate chips

In saucepan over low heat, melt semisweet chips, condensed milk, jam, and butter, stirring constantly. Pour into pie pan. Refrigerate until mixture is thick but soft, about 1½ hours. Form into 1-inch balls. Place on baking sheet lined with waxed paper. In microwavable bowl, melt white chocolate chips on high for 1 minute. Stir. Melt on high for 30 seconds more or until completely melted. Spoon melted chocolate over top of each truffle ball, allowing chocolate to drip slightly down sides of each ball. Refrigerate until chocolate is firm. Store in refrigerator.

Merry Minty Truffles

1¼ cups mint chocolate chips
⅓ cup whipping cream

¼ cup butter
Chocolate sprinkles

In saucepan over medium heat, melt chocolate chips, cream, and butter, stirring constantly. Pour into pie pan. Refrigerate until thick but soft, about 2 hours. Shape into 1-inch balls. Place sprinkles in shallow bowl. Roll balls in sprinkles. Place on baking sheet lined with waxed paper. Let set. Store in tightly covered container in refrigerator.

Double Chocolate Truffles

½ cup whipping cream
1 tablespoon butter
4 squares semisweet baking
  chocolate, broken into pieces

1 (7 ounce) milk chocolate
  candy bar, broken into
  pieces
½ teaspoon almond extract
Finely ground almonds

In saucepan, combine whipping cream and butter. Cook over medium heat, stirring constantly until mixture is very hot. Do not boil. Remove from heat. Add baking chocolate pieces, candy bar pieces, and almond extract. Stir with whisk until smooth. Cover with plastic wrap. Let cool several hours or until mixture is firm enough to handle. Shape into 1-inch balls. Roll in ground almonds. Refrigerate until firm, about 2 hours. Store in tightly covered container in refrigerator.

Peanut Butter Truffles

2 cups milk chocolate chips
½ cup whipping cream
2 tablespoons butter

½ cup creamy peanut butter
¾ cup finely chopped peanuts

In saucepan over low heat, melt chocolate chips, cream, and butter, stirring occasionally. Whisk in peanut butter until blended. Pour into pie pan. Refrigerate until thick but soft, about 1 hour. Shape into 1-inch balls. Roll balls in peanuts. Place on waxed paper. Store in refrigerator.

Marbled Truffles

¾ cup white chocolate chips
½ cup whipping cream, divided
1 teaspoon vanilla
¾ cup semisweet chocolate chips

1 tablespoon butter
1 teaspoon orange extract
¾ cup powdered sugar

In saucepan over low heat, melt white chocolate chips, ¼ cup whipping cream, and vanilla, stirring constantly. Pour into 9x9-inch pan. Refrigerate. In saucepan, melt semisweet chips, butter, and remaining whipping cream over low heat, stirring constantly. Remove from heat. Add extract. Pour chocolate mixture over refrigerated white chocolate mixture. Refrigerate until mixture is thick but soft, about 1 hour. Shape mixture into 1-inch balls. Place powdered sugar in shallow pan. Roll balls in sugar. Place on waxed paper. Store in refrigerator.

When Jesus was born,
God lit up the sky with His glory
for all people to see, but He also made
the star so individuals who were seeking
Him could find Him.

OTHER FAVORITES

Christmas is for children. It must be so
because even the Creator of the universe
was a Child that first Christmas Day.

Popcorn Balls

12 cups popped corn

1½ cups sugar

½ cup brown sugar

1½ cups water

½ teaspoon salt

¾ cup corn syrup

1 teaspoon vanilla

Spread popped corn in large shallow pan. In saucepan, combine sugars, water, salt, corn syrup, and vanilla. Mix well. Cook until candy thermometer reads 260°. Pour over popped corn slowly. Butter hands and form popcorn into balls. Makes about 15 to 20 popcorn balls.

Penuche

2 cups brown sugar
1 cup sugar
1½ cups half-and-half
1½ tablespoons butter

1 teaspoon vanilla
⅛ teaspoon salt
1 cup walnut pieces

Combine sugars, half-and-half, butter, vanilla, and salt in saucepan. Bring to a boil over medium heat until temperature reaches 238°, stirring constantly. Remove from heat. Beat with mixer on medium speed until cool and creamy. Stir in walnuts. Pour onto greased pan to cool.

Eggnog Candy

2 cups sugar
¾ cup eggnog
2 tablespoons light corn syrup

2 tablespoons butter
1 teaspoon vanilla

In saucepan over medium heat, cook sugar, eggnog, corn syrup, and butter, stirring constantly until sugar dissolves. Boil until candy thermometer reads 238°. Pour into bowl. Cool to about 110°. Add vanilla and beat with mixer until thick. Spread into buttered 8x8-inch pan. Score into squares. Refrigerate until firm. Store in refrigerator.

Lemon Drops

2 egg whites, room temperature
¼ teaspoon cream of tartar
⅛ teaspoon salt
⅔ cup sugar

2 tablespoons lemon gelatin
  mix
¾ teaspoon lemon extract

Preheat oven to 200°. Line 2 large cookie sheets with foil. In small bowl with mixer on high speed, beat egg whites, cream of tartar, and salt until soft peaks form. Still beating at high speed, add sugar 2 tablespoons at a time. Add gelatin mix and extract. Beat until stiff peaks form. Drop by level teaspoons onto cookie sheets. Bake for 1 hour and 15 minutes or until set. Cool for 10 minutes. With spatula, carefully loosen and remove drops from foil. Cool completely on wire racks. Store in tightly covered container. Makes 3 dozen.

Christmas Gift Popcorn

1 cup brown sugar
½ cup butter
½ cup light corn syrup
½ teaspoon salt

½ teaspoon vanilla
8 cups popped corn
1½ cups pecan pieces
1½ cups walnut pieces

In 2-quart saucepan over medium heat, melt brown sugar, butter, corn syrup, and salt. Boil for 5 minutes, stirring constantly. Remove from heat. Add vanilla. Pour over popped corn and nuts. Mix well. Spread onto greased baking sheet. Bake at 250° for 60 minutes. Remove from oven. Cool. Break into pieces.

Christmas Mints

6 tablespoons butter
½ cup cocoa
2 cups powdered sugar

3 tablespoons plus 1 teaspoon
whole milk, divided
1 teaspoon vanilla

Filling:

3 ounces cream cheese, softened
2 cups powdered sugar
½ teaspoon vanilla

¼ teaspoon peppermint
extract
Milk

In saucepan, melt butter over low heat. Add cocoa and stir until mixture is smooth. Add powdered sugar, 3 tablespoons milk, and vanilla. Cook over low heat, stirring constantly, until mixture is glossy. Spread half of mixture in buttered 8x8-inch pan. Refrigerate.

For filling, beat cream cheese, powdered sugar, vanilla, and peppermint extract until smooth. Add 2 to 3 teaspoons milk if needed for spreading consistency. Spread cream cheese mixture over chocolate layer in pan. Refrigerate for 10 minutes.

To remaining chocolate mixture in saucepan, add 1 teaspoon milk. Heat over low heat until smooth. Spread over cream cheese mixture in pan. Refrigerate until firm. Cut into squares. Store in refrigerator.

Popcorn Candy

12 cups popped corn
1¼ cups sugar
1¼ cups molasses

½ teaspoon salt
1½ tablespoons butter, melted

Spread popped corn onto buttered pan. Combine sugar, molasses, salt, and melted butter in saucepan. Cook until candy thermometer reads 290°. Pour mixture over popped corn and spread thin, making sure all corn is covered. Cool. Break into pieces.

Orange Balls

½ cup butter, softened
3½ cups powdered sugar
1 (6 ounce) can frozen orange
   juice concentrate

1 (15 ounce) box vanilla
   wafers, crushed
1 cup pecan pieces

Combine butter, powdered sugar, orange juice concentrate, and crushed vanilla wafers in mixing bowl. Blend well then stir in pecans. Chill for 5 to 10 minutes. Form mixture into 1-inch balls. Chill until ready to serve.

Cinnamon Candies

2 cups sugar
1 cup light corn syrup
½ cup water

½ teaspoon red food coloring
½ teaspoon cinnamon oil

In heavy saucepan, combine sugar, corn syrup, and water. Cook until mixture reaches 285°. Remove from heat. Stir in food coloring and cinnamon oil. Pour onto greased pan and cool completely. Break into pieces.

Divinity

4 egg whites, room temperature
½ teaspoon cream of tartar
4 cups sugar

1 cup water
1 cup light corn syrup
2 teaspoons vanilla

Beat egg whites and cream of tartar until stiff peaks form. Boil sugar, water, and corn syrup until temperature reaches 250° on candy thermometer. While constantly beating egg whites, slowly pour half the syrup over them. Boil remaining syrup to 280°. Beat egg whites again while slowly pouring in remaining syrup. Stir in vanilla. Let mixture stand until cool. Drop by teaspoons onto waxed paper.

Cornflake Candy

1 cup sugar
1 cup light corn syrup
½ cup cream

4 cups cornflakes
1 cup flaked coconut
1 cup walnut pieces

In saucepan over medium heat, cook sugar, corn syrup, and cream until candy thermometer reaches 238°. Pour mixture over cornflakes, coconut, and walnuts. Mix thoroughly. Drop by tablespoons onto waxed paper. When cool, store in tightly covered container.

Festive Mints

1 (8 ounce) package cream cheese,
  softened
1 teaspoon mint extract
6⅔ cups powdered sugar

Red, green, and yellow food
  coloring
Sugar

In small mixing bowl, beat cream cheese and mint extract until smooth. Gradually beat in as much powdered sugar as possible. Knead in remaining powdered sugar. Divide mixture into four portions. Tint one pink, one green, and one yellow, leaving one portion white. For each color, shape into 1/2-inch balls. Dip one side of each ball in sugar. Press sugared side into small candy mold; unmold and place on waxed paper. Let stand for 1 hour or until dry before storing in airtight container; refrigerate. May be stored for up to 1 week before serving.

Holiday Mints

3 ounces cream cheese, softened
3 tablespoons butter, softened
½ teaspoon vanilla
Food coloring

¼ teaspoon peppermint
  extract
4 cups powdered sugar
⅓ cup sugar

In large bowl, beat cream cheese, butter, vanilla, food coloring, and peppermint extract on medium speed until smooth. Gradually beat in powdered sugar on low speed until well combined. Place sugar in shallow bowl. Roll 2 teaspoons cream cheese mixture into ball. Roll ball in sugar until coated. Flatten ball with fingers or fork to make small patty. Place patties on baking sheet lined with waxed paper. Refrigerate until firm. Store in refrigerator.

Buttermilk Candy

1 cup buttermilk
1 teaspoon baking soda
2 cups sugar
2 tablespoons light corn syrup

2 tablespoons butter
1 teaspoon vanilla
1 cup pecan pieces

In saucepan, combine buttermilk, baking soda, sugar, corn syrup, and butter. Cook over medium heat, stirring constantly until sugar dissolves and mixture comes to a boil. Reduce heat to low. Cook until candy thermometer reads 238°. Pour into large mixing bowl. Cool to about 110°. Add vanilla and beat on medium speed until mixture is thick. Add pecan pieces. Beat until candy starts to lose its gloss. Spread in buttered 8x8-inch pan. Refrigerate until firm. Cut into squares. Store in refrigerator.

Lollipops

1 cup water	½ teaspoon oil of lemon,
⅓ cup corn syrup	peppermint, or cinnamon
2 cups sugar	Food coloring

Oil lollipop mold and place lollipop sticks in position. Combine water, corn syrup, and sugar in medium saucepan. Cook over medium heat, stirring constantly until sugar dissolves and mixture comes to a boil. Continue cooking until candy thermometer reaches 300°. Remove from heat. Add flavoring and food coloring. Spoon hot mixture into prepared molds. Cool thoroughly. When firm, remove from molds.

Maple Sugar Candy

1 pound maple sugar, softened   ¼ cup hot water
¾ cup light cream   ⅔ cup walnut pieces

Break sugar into pieces. Place in saucepan with cream and water. Bring to a boil. Boil until candy thermometer reaches 238°. Remove from heat. Beat on medium speed until creamy. Add walnut pieces. Pour into buttered 8x8-inch pan. Cool. Cut into squares.

Marshmallow Cups

2 cups milk chocolate chips
2 tablespoons shortening

1 cup marshmallow crème

Line mini muffin baking pans with 18 foil cups. In saucepan over low heat, melt chocolate chips with shortening, stirring constantly. Spoon ½ tablespoon chocolate mixture into each cup, using back of spoon to spread chocolate up sides of each cup. Spoon 1 tablespoon marshmallow crème into each cup. Spoon ½ tablespoon remaining chocolate over each marshmallow cup. Refrigerate until firm.

Peppermints

1½ cups sugar   6 drops oil of peppermint
½ cup boiling water

In saucepan, combine sugar and water, stirring until sugar is dissolved. Cook over medium heat until mixture begins to boil. Boil for 10 minutes. Remove from heat. Add peppermint oil. Beat with mixer on medium speed until mixture is creamy. Drop by teaspoons onto buttered waxed paper. Allow to cool. Store in refrigerator.

Orange Drops

1 cup evaporated milk
3 cups sugar, divided
½ cup orange juice, boiling

¼ teaspoon salt
Zest of 2 oranges
1 cup pecan pieces

In saucepan, combine evaporated milk and 1 cup sugar. Cook until sugar is dissolved. Add boiling orange juice. Blend well. Stir in 2 cups sugar and salt. Bring to a boil. Cover and boil for 3 minutes. Reduce heat to low and cook uncovered without stirring until candy thermometer reaches 238°. Remove from heat. Add zest. Mix well. Let cool. Beat mixture on medium speed until mixture is creamy. Stir in pecans. Drop by teaspoons onto waxed paper. When cool, wrap candies individually in plastic wrap and store at room temperature in tightly covered container.

Cookies and Cream Bonbons

24 chocolate cream-filled cookies
1 (8 ounce) package cream
   cheese, softened

1 cup nonfat dry milk
1 teaspoon vanilla
2 cups powdered sugar

Coarsely chop 12 cookies and set aside. Place remaining 12 cookies in food processor. Process until fine crumbs form. Place crumbs on baking sheet lined with waxed paper. Set aside. Beat cream cheese, milk, and vanilla in medium bowl at medium speed until smooth. Beat in powdered sugar, 1 cup at a time, at low speed until mixture is smooth. Stir in chopped cookies. Refrigerate for 2 hours or until firm. Shape into 1-inch balls. Roll balls in cookie crumb mixture. Store in airtight container in refrigerator.

INDEX

Almond Brittle...65
Almond Butter Toffee..42
Apricot Balls 20
Banana Clusters 18
Brown Sugar Coconut Delights 80
Bull's Eyes...60
Butter Taffy 29
Buttermilk Candy 145
Butterscotch..36
Butterscotch Caramels 35
Butterscotch Delights 33
Butterscotch Divinity...37
Candy Apples 19

Caramel Apples 11
Caramel Nut Cups 50
Caramel Popcorn 40
Caramels 49
Cashew Brittle 61
Cherry Chocolate Logs 15
Cherry Vanilla Nougat 16
Choco-Coconut Bars 72
Chocolate Butter Crunch 92
Chocolate Caramels 34
Chocolate Coconut Bonbons 85
Chocolate-Covered Cherries 22
Chocolate-Covered Raisins 23
Chocolate Cream Candy 93

Chocolate Date Nut Rolls 9

Chocolate-Dipped Strawberries 13

Chocolate Drops 90

Chocolate Nut Squares. 86

Chocolate Peppermints 87

Chocolate Popcorn. 88

Chocolate Pretzels 89

Chocolate Toffee 31

Choco-Peanut Butter Bars 84

Christmas Caramels 41

Christmas Chocolate Truffles 119

Christmas Crunchies 48

Christmas Fudge 96

Christmas Gift Popcorn. 135

Christmas Mints. 136
Christmas Peanuts 52
Christmas Pralines 53
Cinnamon Candies 140
Cocoa Fudge 105
Coconut Almond Bars 76
Coconut Almond Delights 74
Coconut Balls. 77
Coconut Bonbons 78
Coconut Cream Candy 75
Coconut Cream Truffles. 118
Coconut Haystacks 70
Cookie Dough Fudge. 98
Cookies and Cream Bonbons 151

Cornflake Candy 142
Creamed Walnuts. 57
Date Loaf Candy 8
Date-Fig Confections. 12
Divinity 141
Double Chocolate Truffles 126
Double Peanut Butter Chocolate Fudge 102
Double-Decker Fudge 108
Eggnog Candy 133
Eggnog Truffles 120
Fabulous Fudge 100
Festive Mints 143
Fudgy Peanut Butter Balls 116
Glacé Cherries 17

Glacé Nuts 58
Hawaiian Toffee 44
Haystacks 39
Holiday Mints 144
Honey Butter Fudge 103
Layered Chocolate Mints 83
Layered Fudge 114
Lemon Drops 134
Lollipops 146
Maple Fudge 113
Maple Sugar Candy 147
Marbled Truffles 128
Marshmallow Cups 148
Merry Minty Truffles 125

Microwave Brittle. 64
Mississippi Mud Fudge. 95
Mocha Fudge 106
Molasses Taffy 28
Never Fail Fudge 104
Orange Balls. 139
Orange Drops 150
Orange Truffles 122
Peanut Brittle. 67
Peanut Butter Crunchies 55
Peanut Butter Cups 54
Peanut Butter Delights. 59
Peanut Butter Fudge. 97
Peanut Butter Fudge #2 107

Peanut Butter Truffles. 127
Peanut Nougat 56
Pecan Roll 68
Penuche 132
Peppermints. 149
Popcorn Balls 131
Popcorn Candy 138
Quick Fudge 111
Raspberry Truffles 124
Rocky Road Delights 82
Spiced Nuts 63
Sugarplums 21
Sultana Caramels 32
Taffy. 25

Taffy Delight 27
Toffee. 46
Traditional Peanut Brittle. 66
Turtle Fudge. 110
Turtles 47
Velvet Taffy 26
Walnut Fudge. 112
White Chocolate Apricots 14
White Chocolate Truffles 121